BLACK PLANTS

BLACK PLANTS

75 STRIKING CHOICES FOR THE GARDEN

PAUL BONINE

TIMBER PRESS

PORTLAND · LONDON

Photography credits on page 159.

Published in 2009 by Timber Press, Inc.

The Haseltine Building   2 The Quadrant
133 S.W. Second Avenue, Suite 450   135 Salusbury Road
Portland, Oregon 97204-3527   London NW6 6RJ
www.timberpress.com   www.timberpress.co.uk

Printed in China

Library of Congress Cataloging-in-Publication Data

Bonine, Paul.
    Black plants / Paul Bonine. — 1st ed.
       p. cm.
     ISBN 978-0-88192-981-2
   1. Color in gardening. 2. Plants, Ornamental—Color. I. Title.
     SB454.3.C64B66 2009
     635.9'68—dc22
                                              2009005846

A catalog record for this book is also available from the British Library.

KEY TO PLANT CARE SYMBOLS

LIGHT REQUIREMENTS

 SUN
Plant receives six hours or more of direct sun every day.

 PART SUN
Plant receives three to six hours of direct sun every day.

 LIGHT SHADE
Plant receives less than three hours of direct sun and gets dappled sun at other times during the day.

 SHADE
Plant receives little or no direct sun, only dappled sun.

MOISTURE REQUIREMENTS

 HEAVY
Plant needs constantly moist soil.

 MODERATE
Plant needs moderate moisture—the surface of the soil can dry out between waterings.

 LIGHT
Plant tolerates some dryness—the top inch or two of the soil can dry out between waterings.

INTRODUCTION

Black has always been associated with mystery, and dark-leaved and dark-flowered plants—as unnatural as they may seem—are a part of nature that is undeniably alluring. Even an ordinary garden can be transformed by dark foliage and flowers into a canvas with the depth and play of light and shadow as detailed as a painting by a Dutch realist. Many theories exist about why certain plants developed dark-hued foliage and flowers. The compounds responsible for these deep colors, anthocyanins, may act as protection against intense sunlight or they may simply be a genetic trait—an overabundance of pigment that is passed from one generation to the next. Science aside, these plants at the darkest edge of the spectrum have woven their appeal into the soul of gardeners. The plants that appear in this book—which include annuals, perennials, shrubs, and trees, as well as hardy plants and tropicals—will give you the tools to create your own unforgettable scenes of somber beauty.

Actaea simplex (*Atropurpurea* Group) 'Hillside Black Beauty'

'Hillside Black Beauty' bugbane

A regal perennial of dark elegance, this bugbane is hardly the bane of gardeners. Intricate, divided leaves are a lacquered black and as ornate as the carved designs on a piece of Moorish furniture. Supported by a thick dark central stem, the large leaflets are arranged in handsome symmetrical tiers. In late summer to early autumn, towering spikes of soft, white, cylindrical flowers take center stage and are often followed by white berries that remain showy on the dormant winter stems if not taken by birds. This four-foot herbaceous perennial prefers part shade and rich, moist soil; it may not perform at its peak in areas with mild winters.

ZONE 3

'Zwartkop' aeonium

Stunned silence is often the first reaction to this alien-looking succulent. What would such a plant call home? A coral reef? A faraway planet? Actually, it comes from Madeira, the Canary Islands, and North Africa, where so many other plants of unearthly character reside. 'Zwartkop' (Dutch for "black head") bears glossy leaves arranged in perfectly round five-inch-wide rosettes. Its deep hue and bold symmetry make it an instant hit in containers, where it provides an ideal foil for silver- and gray-leaved plants. 'Zwartkop' does best with fast-draining soil mix, with light applications of fertilizer and light water during the growing season.

ZONE 10

Agapanthus inapertus
Lily-of-the-Nile

Gardeners used to the spherical burst of blue flowers common to lily-of-the-Nile are taken aback when they encounter this unusual, deeply hued species. Sturdy thirty-inch stems produce nodding clusters of intensely deep bluish black bell-shaped flowers. Indeed, the intensity of the flower color makes up for what might be seen as a somewhat brooding attitude. A tight, clump-forming deciduous perennial, it is among the cold-hardiest of its clan. Rich, well-drained soil that doesn't get soggy in winter, along with adequate irrigation in summer, suits it best.

ZONE 7

Agonis flexuosa 'Jervis Bay Afterdark'

'Jervis Bay Afterdark' peppermint tree

This spectacular black-leaved form of Australian willow myrtle until recently was little known, but has achieved popularity as a dramatic landscape or container plant in mild and cold climates. Shocking dark leaves on pendant branches absorb and reflect light in an irresistible display. In climates where hard frost is rare it will grow into a graceful weeping tree to eighteen feet tall. Small plants will grow quickly if given rich soil and full sun to very light shade. Its somewhat lax habit may require support to produce a stronger trunk. Peppermint tree can be difficult to root from cuttings.

ZONE 9

Ajuga reptans 'Black Scallop'

'Black Scallop' bugleweed

The tough disposition of common bugleweed is hard to beat, but this form, with glossy, dapper foliage, is exceptional. Its sparkling, concave leaves are arranged in a tight mound that spreads slowly up to one foot wide in several seasons. In early summer, four-inch spikes of indigo flowers rise above the foliage, creating a harmonious effect. Rich, moist soil in part shade to full sun is optimum, but it adapts to dry conditions as it becomes established. In zones 7 and south it remains evergreen—or everblack. Pair it with blue-foliaged shrubs and perennials (like hostas) for gorgeous effects.

ZONE 4

Albizia julibrissin 'Summer Chocolate'

'Summer Chocolate' silk tree

ZONE 6

The full glory of this tree is best experienced in person. At first sight gardeners may stare in awe and think about the trees they could replace with 'Summer Chocolate'. Fine, lacy foliage resembling dark baking chocolate adds to all of the romance and handsome structure that has made silk tree so popular. In late summer perfumed powder-pink flowers create a haze over the foliage; the umbrella-shaped tree can reach twenty feet tall and as wide. The delicious foliage is late to appear in spring so sun-loving early perennials will do well beneath it. 'Summer Chocolate' prefers full sun and well-drained soil that is not too rich.

Alcea rosea 'Nigra'
Black hollyhock

ZONE 4

B lack hollyhock has been treasured by gardeners for more than two hundred years. Best grown from seed, this biennial or short-lived perennial sends up towering five- to eight-foot spires of rich black flowers, centered with light yellow. It looks extraordinary planted in a row against a simple background, such as a weather-worn wooden fence. Black hollyhock will bloom from late June to frost if spent flower spikes are removed. Give it full, hot sun, well-drained soil that is not overly fertile, and good air circulation (to forestall rust as long as possible).

Alternanthera dentata 'Rubiginosa'
Ruby calico plant

R elatively new to the gardening scene, ruby calico plant is a tropical annual that is decidedly luscious. The pointed, angular leaves and stems are saturated in the deepest maroon. For an out-of-this-world container planting, combine with *Coleus* 'Black Magic' or a lime-green cultivar of *Plectranthus argentatus*. 'Rubiginosa' is easily cultivated in rich soil (or any standard potting mixture), as long as it gets regular summer water and fertilizer. Given full sun to very light shade, in one season it will reach a height and width of twenty inches. It is especially at home in sultry, humid climates, making it an excellent choice for the southeastern United States.

ZONE 10

Amorphophallus konjac

Devil's tongue

"Bizarre," "alien," and "unreal" are apt descriptions for this sinister and brazen creature. The enormous, thick stem of devil's tongue, clad in black blotches and stripes, can reach five feet in height and produces a large, finely divided, exotic-looking leaf. Once the tuber attains sufficient girth (which may take several seasons), a six-foot flower bursts out of the ground. The dark brown spadix—which can only be described as lurid—reaches a height of three feet and is surrounded by a glossy, chocolate-colored, rubber-textured, vaselike spathe. This fascinating plant requires patience and woodland conditions with average amounts of water during the summer months.

ZONE 7

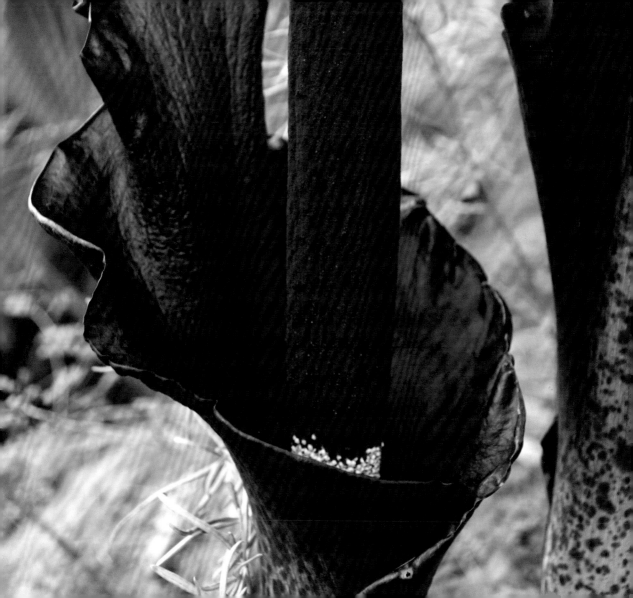

Angelica gigas

Korean angelica

ZONE 5

Korean angelica is a robust and mysterious biennial that performs a bold two-year show in the garden. Lush, large leaves form a rosette in their first season. The following summer, burgundy-ribbed red stems rise from three to six feet tall, branching and displaying curious large buds surrounded by a red-striped papery wrapping. These open to reveal dark purple-red umbels which are irresistible to honey bees, who roam intoxicated through the flower's dark riches collecting pollen. Korean angelica is interesting even after it dies, its skeleton remaining erect and turning a deep wrought-iron black that lasts throughout the winter. Give it full sun to part shade in rich, well-drained soil. It will self-sow in open, disturbed ground.

Anthriscus sylvestris 'Ravenswing'

'Ravenswing' cow parsley

Ordinary cow parsley may not get the pulse racing, but this black selection offers heart-pounding, coffee-hued foliage with a glossy edge. In full sun 'Ravenswing' has a curious maroon sheen, but in shade it remains shadowy and dark. A true biennial, it produces a one-foot clump of rich foliage during its first season. The following year it can reach thirty inches, topped by ghostly white umbels. This precious self-sower tucks its black wings between other plants, creating unplanned but welcome combinations. Volunteer seedlings, which are conspicuous from an early age, may be moved or dispatched as the gardener likes. Give the plant loose, friable soil in full sun to shade with average amounts of water.

ZONE 6

Aquilegia vulgaris 'Clementine Dark Purple'

'Clementine Dark Purple' columbine

ZONE 3

This jaunty selection of the common European columbine takes the form of a giant, purple-black pinwheel. Gone are the spurs that soar like a shooting star, replaced by row upon row of outward-pointing petals on outward-pointing flowers. The deep grape color of the flowers makes them seem bigger than they really are, so that the plant appears to have an abundance of bloom. Like other columbines, this twenty-inch-tall strain bears typical lacy blue foliage reminiscent of a maidenhair fern. Columbines self-seed readily, but if you grow more than one strain, you're likely to get intermediate forms. 'Clementine Dark Purple' needs full sun to light dappled shade and reliable water through the summer.

Arisaema aff. *griffithii*

Griffith's cobra lily

T he most appropriate site for this unique jack-in the-pulpit relative would be the deep woods where fairies and elves reside. Rising directly from the ground, the spathe, or hood, of Griffith's cobra lily is rich mahogany-brown striped in green. It folds over itself, obscuring the deep brown spadix that stands inside. This flower is at its peak in mid-April to May; after a week or two it is followed by a single, large, three-lobed leaf that stands tall and bold for the remainder of the summer. Give this plant shade, humus-rich soil, and plenty of moisture.

ZONE 7

Arisaema concinnum

Chinese cobra lily

Native from the eastern Himalayas into Sichuan, this cobra lily is one of the showiest species of a group of woodland perennials also known as lords and ladies. The curious inflorescence rises directly from the ground and opens almost immediately. The reddish black spathe, striped in white, encloses the deep black spadix which is waiting to be pollinated. Large, green palmate leaves follow the flower's appearance and persist handsomely through summer. Spreading by stolons, Chinese cobra lily can reach five feet in height and needs rich woodland soil with ample moisture and dappled shade.

ZONE 7

Asarum maximum

Large wild ginger

Vigilance and curiosity are required to discover the glory of this small evergreen woodland perennial. The flowers of large wild ginger are tucked unobtrusively at the base of its glossy heart-shaped leaves. Ornate tubular cups have a ring of white fur at the base of each petal and beyond the black throat. Each flower is so neat it's as if it was fashioned out of felt to decorate the brim of a hat. The plant needs rich soil with a high humus content that drains well but retains moisture. It can reach six inches tall and over time will form colonies.

ZONE 6

Begonia 'Non-Stop Mocha Mix'

'Non-Stop Mocha Mix' begonia

The dark leaves of 'Mocha Mix' tuberous begonias offer the kind of over-the-top quality that gardeners crave during the hot summer months. Double to single flowers come in a brilliant range of colors from whites tinted with green to fully double blossoms in outrageous crimsons, oranges, and yellows. The dark-tinted leaves, veined in green, are the perfect foil to enhance these molten colors and add substance and depth. Plants need part to full shade in rich, well-drained soil that remains moist. Occasional applications of fertilizer will propel the show well into autumn.

ZONE 8

'Night Rider' camellia

A nthocyanins are the chemical compounds that impart the darkest colors to plants. 'Night Rider' is so steeped in these pigments that even the *roots* are blood red. A single late-blooming variety, 'Night Rider' bears flowers whose petals have an unusual rubbery texture. The just-opened flowers are shaded with black, then ease to oxblood-red as they mature. The new growth of this handsome, moderate-growing shrub emerges deep red before maturing to a glossy black green. Reaching ten feet high and wide, it prefers part shade and well-drained soil with consistent moisture.

ZONE 7

Canna 'Australia'
'Australia' canna

Cannas are both the essence of tropical opulence and an age-old standard for the summer garden. The bold burgundy-black leaves of 'Australia' are especially dramatic. Held at an angle parallel to the stems, they unfurl into upturned shields that clothe thick stalks up to eight feet tall. In midsummer, rich red flowers erupt from the top, dancing like the flames of a tiki torch. A semi-tender perennial, 'Australia' will form large colonies if given full sun and rich, moist soil. In areas colder than zone 8, lift and store the rhizomes after the first sharp frost in autumn.

ZONE 8

Capsicum 'Black Pearl'

'Black Pearl' ornamental pepper

ZONE 10

I t didn't take gardeners long to realize that peppers weren't just vegetables but extraordinarily pretty plants as well. 'Black Pearl' is an ornamental variety with shining black foliage and stems on a dense and rounded twenty-inch-tall plant. The glory of this plant is the perfectly round, small black peppers that appear in profusion; first glossy black then red and finally orange, they are a knockout against the deep-hued leaves. 'Black Pearl' pepper likes full sun in a very hot location and rich soil and ample water during the growing season. For a firelike contrast in mixed containers pair it with the smoky white foliage of *Senecio viravira* and orange-flowered *Cuphea* 'David Verity'.

Clematis recta 'Purpurea'

'Purpurea' upright virgin's bower

Intense mahogany-black stems and foliage erupt from the ground in early spring on this easily grown and charming herbaceous clematis. As it inches skyward the non-twining stems arch then ramble several yards, the leaves mellowing to deep green. In May and June a blizzard of starry white flowers appears in a frothy haze, often peering through and over neighboring plants. In rich, moist soil this clematis may be cut to the ground in midsummer to enjoy another dramatic emergence of the dark leaves. Pair with boldly variegated *Euphorbia characias* 'Tasmanian Tiger' to enhance the depth of color in the clematis.

ZONE 4

Colocasia escultenta 'Black Magic'
'Black Magic' elephant ear

E lephant ears are the ultimate in bold tropical-leaved perennials, but 'Black Magic' elevates this plant to a whole new level. Sumptuous, thick rubbery leaves and stems are a saturated licorice black, viewed perfectly through leaves that face outward and hang like brazen shields. The visual impact of a well-grown plant is undeniably breathtaking. This form of elephant ear requires protection in all but the most tropical climates, and is at home in moist soil and even shallow water. Dig and store the large bulb before the first hard freeze, and replant in spring when truly warm weather has returned.

ZONE 9

Coprosma 'Black Cloud'

'Black Cloud' coprosma

'B lack Cloud' is a fine-textured evergreen shrub
that does well in mild climates, with glossy leaves
shaded in black and a branching pattern of symmetric
discipline. In youth its habit is low and spreading
and gives little hint of its ultimate form which is tall
rather than broad. The fine black foliage mimics a
thundercloud in a stormy afternoon sky. Specimens
left unpruned will form a conical shape to four feet
tall and four feet wide at the base. 'Black Cloud'
prefers full sun to light shade in well-drained soil,
including sand, and is very tolerant of dry conditions
when established.

ZONE 8

Cosmos atrosanguineus
Chocolate cosmos

N ature's remarkable serendipity has given chocolate cosmos legendary status among gardeners. The chocolate- and mahogany-tinged flowers even exude a fragrance of rich, unsweetened baker's chocolate. The entire handsome plant is shadowed in dark colors, with black petioles and leaves outlined in mahogany, all contributing to the extraordinary design of this Mexican perennial. Unlike other cosmos and similar to the closely related dahlia, it forms a tuberous root system and may be lifted and stored in climates colder than zone 8. Replant in spring in rich, well-drained soil, with full sun in a hot aspect, and provide average amounts of water to sustain this remarkable treasure. Zone 8, zone 7 with protection.

ZONE 7, 8

Dahlia 'Bishop of Llandaff'

'Bishop of Llandaff' dahlia

ZONE 8

Dark-leaved dahlias are not dependent on the size or gaudiness of their flowers—their foliage is just as dazzling. One of the most dashing and distinct of all dark-leaved dahlia cultivars, 'Bishop of Llandaff' is a compact variety that has been grown in gardens for over fifty years. Double flowers are deep velvet red like a noble's robes and are displayed over intricate glossy foliage. A particularly profuse bloomer, it has flowers that rise on strong stems to 20 inches tall. It does well in rich, well-drained soil with ample summer moisture and blooms continuously from late July to October. Dig and store tubers after the first sharp frost in autumn if you garden in zones colder than 8.

Dahlia 'Karma Chocolate'

'Karma Chocolate' dahlia

This dark-hued treasure of a dahlia would be perfectly complemented by trees dripping with Spanish moss and garden beds surrounded by wrought-iron walls—in other words, the sort of setting in which one of Anne Rice's blood-sucking characters would feel at home. Huge, fully double flowers are velvet-red with overtones of black, and can grow up to five inches wide. Its glossy black foliage is echoed on midnight stems. 'Karma Chocolate' is a treat that belongs in every garden where a little decadence is required. Use it as the centerpiece of a planting featuring deep maroon flowers and foliage.

ZONE 8

Delphinium 'Chocolate'

'Chocolate' delphinium

With this unusual black-flowered delphinium, the undisputed queen of the perennial border offers yet another color. Delphiniums are towering floral powerhouses and this variety does not disappoint. Smoky black flowers line its tall stems and make it an ideal subtle backdrop for the dusky blue leaves of *Rosa glauca*. It can also be underplanted with the most brown of all sedges, *Carex comans* 'Red'. Rich soil that has been well-amended, compost, a touch of lime, and full sun are what help this delphinium thrive.

Dianthus 'Black and White Minstrels'

'Black and White Minstrels' carnation

This is an annual carnation that bucks the ideal of double-pink flowers and instead produces fully double white-lace-tipped petals with interiors of rich black. 'Black and White Minstrels' is easy to grow in full sun and well-drained soil, and is showy in mixed containers or beds. It also produces a continuous supply of exquisite cut flowers on fifteen-inch-long stems with a powerful and long-lasting clove scent. In combination with night-scented *Nicotiana* you can create a twenty-four-hour wave of fragrance: carnation clove during the day and sweet drifting cologne at night.

ANNUAL

Dianthus barbatus nigrescens 'Sooty'

'Sooty' sweet William

ZONE 4

Sweet Williams are cottage garden favorites that have been around for centuries. Most of them, however, come in conventional shades of pink, red, mauve, and white. Not this one. It is difficult not to envy a honey bee that gets to land on the sumptuous velvet pillows of the deep black-red-flowered 'Sooty'. The flower's intense color is enhanced by matching maroon-red foliage. 'Sooty' is a short-lived perennial forming a clump that can reach twenty inches tall and as wide in full sun and well-drained soil.

Dracula diabola
Devil's dracula orchid

A rare species of the most sinister genus of orchids, *Dracula diabola* was discovered late in the twentieth century and is only found in one isolated, mist-shrouded valley in Colombia. Three mahogany-red petals open to reveal an interior mottled with brown. Each petal terminates in a long tail, the chief reason for its name diabola, which is Latin for "devil." It is fussy about its requirements for even temperatures and humidity, making it a wicked delight best left to the collector. If, however, you can come up with a reasonable facsimile of conditions in an Andean cloud forest—constantly cool and moist—then this diabolical gem will thrive.

ZONE 11

HOUSEPLANT/ GREENHOUSE

Dracula vampira
Vampire's dracula orchid

It is altogether fitting that this orchid is native to one tall, remote, and misty mountain in Peru. Dracula orchids are best known for their bizarre flowers. Three large petals or sepals are veined with black and white lines, each terminating in a long, midnight-black tail. The interior of the flowers is no less sinister with yellow stripes that radiate from a central white to light pink pouch, reminiscent of a small coffin. 'Bela Lugosi' is a clone that produces flowers which are even more dramatic than the plain species. Dracula orchids require temperatures cooler than most hothouse varieties and are most suitable for the collector.

ZONE 11

HOUSEPLANT/ GREENHOUSE

Dracunculus vulgaris

Voodoo lily

Voodoo lilies are sinister but fascinating bulbs that originated near the Mediterranean but haunt gardens throughout the world. Also known as carrion flower, it first appears as a group of palmate leaves with irregular lobes, but it is the very large flower that steals the show. A rippling spathe with an interior the color of raw meat unfurls in a graceful shield that surrounds the jet black spadix, which can be as long as thirty inches. Pollinated by flies, the freshly opened flower casts a vile, powerful fragrance of rotten flesh, which thankfully disappears in several hours. It prefers little water during the summer months, part shade in average well-drained soil, and is best suited to a location where it may be appreciated but not smelled.

ZONE 5

Epipactis gigantea 'Serpentine Night'

'Serpentine Night' giant stream orchid

T his is one of the very few orchids that is grown for its striking foliage rather than its exotic flowers. Chocolate-colored leaves and stems rise to twenty inches tall and in early summer are topped by elegant but subtle flowers of green and caramel. 'Serpentine Night' is a selection of giant stream orchid that is native to moist, partly shaded locations in the mountains of northern California. It appreciates the same conditions in a garden where it will slowly form a clump. It is winter deciduous and remarkably hardy to cold considering its origin.

ZONE 5

Fritillaria persica
Persian fritillary

N ative to mountainous areas of the Middle East, this stately bulb creates a symmetrical form as sophisticated and beautiful as Arabic architecture. Strap-shaped powder-blue leaves line three-foot stems, each curling at the tip. Remarkable one-foot-long chocolate bells float above the foliage, suspended on wiry stems in a conical arrangement. The entire plant, including stems and flowers, is dusted in what appears to be a fine powder, adding a dreamlike effect that enhances the magical quality of this cold-hardy bulb. During summer it likes full sun and well-drained, enriched soil that is allowed to become dry, and it performs best in climates that deliver a pronounced winter chill.

ZONE 5

Geranium phaeum 'Samobor'
'Samobor' mourning widow

A soft but brooding hardy geranium that is also known as the mourning widow, 'Samobor' is a dark-colored selection of this extraordinarily tough perennial. A dark brown chevron decorates each palm-shaped leaf, and in mid-spring dime-sized, purple-shaded black flowers dance above the foliage which spreads to form large patches up to eighteen inches tall and two feet wide. 'Samobor' is long-lived and thrives in part to full shade; it prefers rich soil with steady irrigation in the hottest months. Established plants will endure dry shade, but will not look their best.

ZONE 4

Gynura bicolor

Velvet plant

T his spectacular yet uncommon perennial is worth
seeking out. Velvet plants are members of the
daisy family, and are best known for their bold furry
gray-black leaves that are lobed at unusual angles
and sport veins of conspicuous white. Each leaf is
up to eighteen inches long and ten inches wide.
Native to the Himalayas, this perennial spreads to six
feet wide and towers up to ten feet tall. In late summer
it is topped with golden orange daisies, and can form
a dramatic stand in the back of a perennial border.
Velvet plants prefer full sun to part shade in rich soil
that remains moist during the growing season.

ZONE 6

Helleborus ×hybridus

Lenten rose

Winter has barely begun to unleash its grip when hellebores reach their crescendo, gripping gardeners the world over with their beauty and tough disposition. Hybridizers have touched this genus with magic, creating flowers in a blizzard of colors and forms including rich black. Its stems and calyx are stained chocolate-brown as they rise and reveal one-inch flowers with a waxy sheen. The great glory and advantage of blooming so early is that the cool days of late winter and early spring add to the length of the flower show. They relish well-drained soil that is moist in summer but never boggy.

Hemerocallis 'Night Wings'
'Night Wings' daylily

ZONE 3

Daylilies are among the most beloved and pervasive perennials in the United States. Breeders have focused intently on these hardy workhorses and have produced an astonishing range of colors and forms. 'Night Wings' is a triumph with large flowers of rich mahogany surrounding a golden yellow throat for vivid contrast. Combining golden-flowered yarrow, ornamental grasses, and daylilies creates a natural meadow effect that is the essence of summer. A moderately tall growing variety can reach twenty-two inches and forms a clump of soft green arching leaves. Daylilies prefer to start life in rich soil with supplemental water during stretches of dry weather. Once established they are tough and very long-lived perennials.

Hermodactylus tuberosus
Snakeshead iris

S nakeshead iris, whose common name alludes to the resemblance of its flower buds to serpents' heads, is an infrequently seen bulb native to the Mediterranean. Grassy leaves emerge in winter and extend to eighteen inches tall, but are delicate enough not to hide the curious—and slightly sinister—flowers that arrive in April and May on one-foot-tall stems. The petals are primarily a light translucent green, with falls that point downward and are licorice-black. This bulb is found in well-drained, somewhat gritty soils and appreciates conditions that are dry in summer. Snakeshead iris may easily be grown in containers in colder regions.

ZONE 7

Heuchera 'Obsidian'

'Obsidian' alumroot

The illusionist illustrator M. C. Escher could have designed this heuchera, whose wavy, scalloped leaves are so dark they seem to absorb almost all light. Starry white flowers, less prominent than the foliage, rise to eighteen inches in early summer on deeply colored stems. In light shade, 'Obsidian' is highly sculptural when paired with the arching leaves of golden Japanese forest grass (*Hakonechloa macra* 'All Gold'). For those who prefer color harmonies, it becomes a pool of midnight beneath maroon-leaved barberries (*Berberis thunbergii* cultivars) or purple-leaved smoketree (*Cotinus coggygria* cultivars). Light shade to full sun and rich, well-draining fertile soil that retains moisture will encourage robust growth.

ZONE 5

Ipomoea batatas 'Ace of Spades'

'Ace of Spades' ornamental sweet potato

This cultivar is an arresting variety of the sweet potato vine that has become an indispensable annual for gardeners. Bold heart-shaped leaves of intense coal black decorate vigorous trailing annual vines that are equally at home in containers or as seasonal groundcovers. Unperturbed by heat and humidity, it flourishes with minimal care and creates a stunning backdrop for other flowers. In ideal conditions stems may grow up to four feet a year. During the season tubers are formed in the soil and may be removed in autumn and stored to be replanted the following spring.

Ipomoea batatas 'Blackie'

'Blackie' ornamental sweet potato

This trailing annual, which took the gardening world by storm when it first appeared, has palmate leaves that resemble spooky hands, and is one of the deepest true black foliage plants. The deeply incised texture of this foliage makes it striking even from a distance and is ideal backed with vivid acid green leaves and hot-colored flowers. This tropical but non-twining vine (it is indeed a relative of the edible sweet potato) shines in containers, spilling out to three feet in a single season. Full sun and rich, moist soil will send this opulent plant speeding along.

ZONE 9

Iris 'Black Gamecock'

'Black Gamecock' Louisiana iris

This vigorous and spectacular selection of Louisiana iris has immense flowers of deep purple with tones of black near the base of each petal. 'Black Gamecock' is a tall-growing cultivar with thirty-inch-long stems which support the six-inch-wide flowers. Louisiana iris may be thought of as the American equivalent of Japanese iris, similar in flower shape and conditions of cultivation. Native to moist places from Texas east to South Carolina, it is not common, and the largest populations are found in the Bayou State of Louisiana. A vigorous easy-going perennial, it should be used more frequently in gardens.

ZONE 5

Iris chysographes 'Black Form'
Black iris

F rom a distance, the flowers of this moisture-loving iris from western China could be mistaken for a hovering group of deep black butterflies. Upon closer inspection the flower form of this unusual black-flowered iris is remarkably detailed. Tiny threads of gold spread from the center of the downward-pointing petals like fine embroidery. This outstanding perennial is hardy to cold and rises to twenty inches tall in bloom, forming large grass green clumps in full sun. Continuously moist soil suits it best; in fact, it makes an ideal choice for stream-side planting. Winter deciduous.

ZONE 4

Leptinella squalida 'Platt's Black'

'Platt's Black' brass buttons

'Platt's Black' is a Lilliputian groundcover with intricate leaves reminiscent of a fern but cast in charcoal black. Densely packed leaves form small mounds which will spread to form weed-smothering patches in rich soil with ample moisture. Full sun intensifies the color of the leaves which are a rich backdrop to the yellow buttons that rise on wiry three-inch-tall stems. Although you wouldn't guess it at first, this perennial is a close relative of daisies, and native to New Zealand (whose flora seems to abound in dark-leaved plants), where it clings to moist mountains slopes.

Maxillaria schunkeana

Schunke's maxillaria

This small beauty from the coastal rain forests of Brazil is one of the most truly black orchids, and blooms for an unusually extended period. Small half-inch flowers are waxy and glossy black with four rounded petals. Thriving in the mossy branches of jungle trees, in bloom it may be seen peering out like many small black eyes. Humid, constantly moist conditions and a planting medium that retains water but at the same time drains freely are needed if the plant is to thrive. Flowers appear from spring well into autumn.

ZONE 11

HOUSEPLANT/ GREENHOUSE

Nemophila menziesii 'Penny Black'

'Penny Black' baby blue eyes

Covering the ground beneath oaks and pines from southern California to western Oregon, this charming wildflower produces bowl-shaped one-inch flowers dotted on the interior with black. 'Penny Black' is a form that connects the dots and forms a single black eye in the center of each. This plant is a spring ephemeral and a true annual, and may easily be grown in containers where it will produce a copious supply of black-eyed flowers until truly hot weather arrives. It will reseed reliably in sandy soil where there is little competition from other plants.

ANNUAL

Ophiopogon planiscapus 'Nigrescens'
Black mondo grass

Black mondo grass has remarkable ebony foliage and is not a grass at all, but a member of the lily family. The evergreen leaves of 'Nigrescens' are arranged in dense arching clumps that curl at the tips with a ribbonlike quality. It deserves a place in virtually all parts of the garden because of its tolerance of full, hot sun or dense shade, and moist or more droughty soils. In early summer small scapes of white flowers are tucked within the foliage, followed by glossy black berries. Regular irrigation during the warmest months will speed growth of this remarkable plant.

ZONE 7

Papaver somniferum 'Black Peony'

'Black Peony' bread seed poppy

Bread seed poppies (occasionally also known as peony-flowered poppies) are age-old favorites for the annual garden. Deep-black-flowered forms are the most enchanting with petals as glossy as cellophane. They are sometimes fringed at the tips as in single-flowered varieties, or rounded and packed into a double form as are many of the best black strains. Bread seed poppies are wonderful as cut flowers; cauterize the stems in hot water as soon as they are cut. Sow seed directly in soil that has been warmed by the spring sun. Seedlings resent competition from other plants and achieve their greatest dimension in open, rich, friable soil with consistent moisture.

ANNUAL

Pennisetum alopecuroides 'Moudry'

'Moudry' fountain grass

Quite unlike other forms of fountain grass, 'Moudry' is an altogether larger plant with leaves that are wider and glossier green. Deep black brushes that look as if they were meant for an autumn painter appear much later than other selections. Displayed on thick upright stems, they resist toppling and do not arch—all the better to see them backlit by the lowering autumn sun. 'Moudry' does well with rich to average soil with average amounts of water in full sun or even a surprising amount of shade. It can reach two feet in height and width. Semi-evergreen.

ZONE 5

Phormium tenax 'Platt's Black'

'Platt's Black' New Zealand flax

New Zealand flax has taken North America by storm as a perennial for warm climates or an annual where the temperature drops below 10° F. Vertical, spiky leaves have a single pleat in the center and rise to a height of three feet on this very dark cultivar. Rich black leaves are glossy on the surface and have a chalky film on the back, giving a crisp architectural effect. In rich soil with ample moisture and full sun, 'Platt's Black' will form a substantial clump in only one season. Ideal as the focal point for containers, it also may be massed in beds to create a dramatic textural effect.

ZONE 8

Phyllostachys nigra
Black bamboo

T he word bamboo conjures such varied images as Chinese forests, grazing pandas, and the simple grace of Asian architecture. Black bamboo is one of the most impressive of this enormous group of true grasses. Yellow-green culms rise from this running variety and in their second season begin to turn to a glossy black. A mature grove draped in willowy leaves atop these black canes is a sight to behold. This cold-hardy bamboo may also be grown in large containers with average amounts of water and protection from intense sun and heat. Black bamboo can reach twenty feet in height and will spread quickly to encompass an area up to two hundred square feet.

ZONE 7

Physocarpus 'Diablo'
'Diablo' common ninebark

Ninebark is a tough, utilitarian shrub, but 'Diablo' is a dark delight. Finely toothed leaves the color of coal turn fiery shades of orange and red in autumn. A moderate-growing shrub reaching six feet tall and as wide, it adds depth and contrast where a resilient plant is required. Able to withstand cold and drought when established, it needs rich soil for robust growth and prospers in full sun to light shade. Flat umbels of small white flowers tinted pink appear in late spring to early summer. It partners well with the fine texture of *Miscanthus sinensis* 'Morning Light' and the smoky leaves of *Sedum* 'Bertram Anderson'.

ZONE 5

'County Park Dwarf' kohuhu

'County Park Dwarf' is an extraordinary broad-leaved evergreen shrub native to New Zealand where it is known as kohuhu. Glossy, wavy leaves emerge green on this compact, slow-growing shrub before changing slowly to purple and then black. For several months in summer it produces this dramatic two-toned effect. Only reaching three feet tall, it slowly spreads just as wide. Excellent resistance to salt spray makes this tender shrub a natural for mild-climate seaside gardens. It is easy care, needing only well-drained soil with occasional water, making it a good choice for use in containers. Established plants will tolerate very dry conditions.

ZONE 8

Primula auricula
Auricula

The most cherished of all primroses, auriculas are the show horses of the alpine plant world. Their distinction comes from the myriad colors in which their flowers may appear. Black, brown, and true gray are all seen, and most exquisite are the forms with a white powdery bloom called farina that may cover the entire plant, including the flowers, to give it a wonderful softness. Auriculas range from show-quality plants that are cosseted under glass, to protect them from the vagaries of weather, to tougher border varieties that may be grown in the ground. They require a cool climate to really thrive.

Pseuderanthemum atropurpureum

Purple false eranthemum

T he love affair with tropical foliage continues, and gardeners especially seem to gravitate to plants from the farthest jungles to satiate their desire. This bold plant native of Java is distantly related to bear's breeches (*Acanthus mollis*) and flaunts large exotic leaves of intense eggplant-purple lightly striped with white or green. Small but vivid rose-colored flowers appear from the tips from midsummer to frost. Enjoying full sun to light shade, it thrives in steamy summer climates where it can grow quickly up to two feet tall and as wide in a growing season. Its bold texture makes it a perfect container companion with *Colocasia* 'Black Magic'.

ZONE 10

Ranunculus ficaria 'Brazen Hussy'

'Brazen Hussy' false celandine

ZONE 5

There must have been a twinkle in the eye of plantsman Christopher Lloyd when he christened this haughty little buttercup. Emerging in late winter, the arrow-shaped leaves of 'Brazen Hussy' are deep black with an oily sheen of blue when viewed in indirect light. Weeks after the foliage appears, copious three-inch-tall shiny electric yellow flowers spread like sunshine across the plant. 'Brazen Hussy' is a summer-dormant perennial that forms colonies in seasonally moist soil. In climates warmer than zone 7 it may truly become brazen by multiplying at a rapid rate. Beware of the plain-leaved form of this species—it can become an almost ineradicable pest.

Rhododendron 'Ebony Pearl'

'Ebony Pearl' rhododendron

Flowers first—that's what the majority of gardeners consider when they include a rhododendron in their garden. This extraordinary variety, by contrast, keeps the attention focused directly on its dramatic shadowy black foliage. 'Ebony Pearl' works well as a dark focal point in the corner of a woodland garden, and its shadowy form is best shown above a brightly leaved groundcover such as brilliant green *Sedum reflexum* 'Angelina'. It is best-suited to dappled shade, rich, moist, humus-enriched soil, and regular water in fast-draining soil during the driest months. Fertilize with an acid-loving mix after the flowers drop.

ZONE 5

Rosa 'Louis XIV'
'Louis XIV' rose

In the nineteenth century Victorians were said to have gone mad in their craze for hybrid perpetual roses (large, hardy, vigorous roses that bloom repeatedly). 'Louis XIV' is one of them, and is a very small shrub with fully double but dainty flowers of rich velvety red with the soft fragrance of lemon. Each petal is pointed at the tip and scrolled under at the base. Its small stature—only two feet tall and as wide—makes it perfect for containers or tight locations. Light repeat bloom continues throughout the season. Rich soil, average amounts of water, full sun, and good air circulation will make this royal rose thrive.

ZONE 6

Salix gracilostylis var. melanostachys
Black pussy willow

A proverbial black sheep—or cat—in the world of willows, the black pussy willow replaces sleek silver catkins with dramatic sooty black. Studded on smooth tan stems they elongate as the days lengthen, eventually revealing showy orange anthers when they bloom. As with all willows, the male form will be the showiest and is easily forced indoors, thus allowing you to create goth-themed arrangements just as winter gives way to spring. This is a carefree shrub for moist locations in full sun. Growing seven feet tall and as wide, it may be pruned to limit its size, which is probably a good idea in most gardens.

ZONE 4

Salpiglossis 'Chocolate Pot'

'Chocolate Pot' painted tongue

Salpiglossis, or painted tongue as they are better known, are dream annuals suited to mild summer climates. Not as popular today as they used to be, they deserve to be more widely grown. 'Chocolate Pot' is a seed strain that comes true with decadent dark funnel-shaped flowers. Equally remarkable are the velvety texture of the flowers and the exquisite contrasting veining. Salpiglossis are closely related to petunias and hail from Chile, where they bloom in the cool spring and early summer. Reaching twenty inches tall, 'Chocolate Pot' will produce scapes of flowers until frost in moist rich soil with average amounts of water and protection from high heat.

Salvia discolor

Andean silver-leaf sage

A ndean silver-leaf sage is an extraordinary sage with a gloomy demeanor. Jet black flowers bloom from pewter calyxes and are held against a backdrop of rounded silver leaves and downy white stems. The sticky leaves exude an oil that prevents the loss of water in its native arid home. This tender salvia makes an ideal seasonal container plant. It may be paired with black mondo grass and *Heuchera* 'Obsidian' for contrasts of silver, black, and iron. It will reach two feet in height and width in full sun to very light shade and well-drained soil.

ZONE 10

Sambucus 'Black Lace'
'Black Lace' elderberry

'Black Lace' is an elderberry with a burlesque edge, its fine, filigreed, true black leaves spreading horizontally in a high-drama performance. In early summer, eight-inch-wide creamy white flowers arranged in an umbel are as delicate as white lace, further softening the display. A vigorous deciduous shrub, 'Black Lace' prefers a spotlight of hot sun but is hardy to cold, and is adaptable to many different soils. It is fast-growing in mild climates but a bit more restrained where the growing season is shorter. It may be hard pruned in early spring. Underplant with *Lysimachia nummularia* 'Aurea' to highlight the brooding deep leaves of this shrub.

ZONE 3

Scabiosa 'Ace of Spades'

'Ace of Spades' scabious

T his form of annual pin cushion flower offers a depth of color unknown in its perennial counterparts. Densely packed flowers are velvet black with just a hint of deep maroon, and appear at the end of long stems. Reaching twenty inches tall, they are wonderful hardy annuals for containers or for spots in a perennial border, and their stunning flowers are also good in small summer bouquets. They prefer full sun and rich, well-drained soil with average amounts of water during the growing season, and may be sown directly into the ground after all danger of frost has passed.

ANNUAL

Sedum 'Black Jack'
'Black Jack' stonecrop

Texture has always played a role in the appeal of succulents, but for those cultivated in cold climates, foliage color was always somewhat limited. Enter 'Black Jack', a recently released variety that is set to become a star. Powdery succulent foliage as dark as spades provides dramatic contrast to umbels of rose-red flowers that appear in late summer. A cold-hardy deciduous perennial, it can reach ten inches tall and as wide in rich, well-drained soil with little supplemental irrigation. 'Black Jack' is ideal for the front of borders or rockeries.

ZONE 4

'Dark Star' coleus

ZONE 10

Sumptuous black leaves with a wrinkled surface give this dramatic coleus added substance and make it a bold focal point in containers or bedding designs. Its lightly scalloped edges add further architectural appeal. 'Dark Star' bulks up quickly in rich, moist soil and is tolerant of full sun in even the most torrid climates. Silver, chartreuse, orange, red, and yellow are ideal colors to take advantage of the rich backdrop of this supreme foliage annual. 'Dark Star' will grow up to eighteen inches tall and wide. Like all coleus, 'Dark Star' can be propagated by simply rooting cuttings in water.

Solenostemon 'Inky Fingers'
'Inky Fingers' coleus

T his is a playful, animated coleus with leaves shaped like small hands that have been pressed on a pad of black ink. The effect is cartoonish, and as this compact and tightly branched coleus grows it forms a veritable crowd of ink-stained palms. It is best-suited to full sun to shade in rich soil. Combining 'Inky Fingers' with sleek grasses or large-leaved plants in containers emphasizes the detail that makes it a frivolous wonder. No one ever said that gardening has to be serious all the time.

Streliztia nicholai

Giant bird-of-paradise

The distinct fan shape of giant bird-of-paradise makes it easy to recognize from a distance, and though it is not quite as well-known as its orange- and blue-flowered counterpart, it is no less dramatic. Forming multiple trunks to twenty feet tall, this close relative of the banana shares the same bold leaves and has unusual flowers appearing at the base of each leafy fan. A sharply pointed black bud emerges, and as it opens white petals rise up like the head feathers of a cockatoo. It thrives in full sun and sandy soil with occasional irrigation, but is restricted to the mildest zones because of its intolerance of cold temperatures.

ZONE 9

Tacca chantrieri
Bat flower

W hat strange twist in evolutionary fate could have caused the formation of such a foreign and unlikely flower? The bat flower or cat's whiskers, as it is known, is not an invention of science fiction but a plant native to the jungles of Thailand. A long black chord of a stem suspends this flower, which is actually a group of flowers, in a rubbery black sepal. Protruding from the side of each flower are long stringlike cords. Your first encounter might be fright— or laughter. This is a tropical perennial that lives on moist cliffs in shady ravines, although it is surprisingly amenable to hothouse culture.

ZONE 10

**HOUSEPLANT/
GREENHOUSE**

Trillium chloropetalum 'Volcano'

'Volcano' giant wake robin

Glistening wake robins or trilliums are among the quintessential signs of spring. *Trillium chloropetalum*, the giant wake robin native to the Northwest coast of North America, comes in a range of colors—some approaching molasses. 'Volcano' is a floriferous selection with dark but vivid red flowers. Just as fetching as the flowers are the dark spots or checks that decorate each of the three large leaves. Woodland conditions, shade, and soil that is high in organic matter and retains moisture will suit this plant best. 'Volcano' will grow up to two feet tall and as wide.

ZONE 5

Tulipa 'Queen of Night'

'Queen of Night' tulip

With the darkest flower color of any hybrid, 'Queen of Night' produces goblets of aubergine-black with a satin gloss. This single-flowered late variety has a tough disposition and will persist in the right location for years, multiplying slowly to form colonies. 'Queen of Night' is most commonly used as a beacon of contrast in mass plantings of lighter-hued varieties. Its long two-foot stems make it a marvelous cut flower. It likes rich, well-drained soil, ideally loam, in full sun or the light shade found under deciduous trees.

ZONE 3

Veratrum nigrum
Black false hellebore

As it rises from the ground and unfurls its perfectly crisp accordion leaves, black false hellebore looks as if it was fashioned from stone by an artist from antiquity. In early summer and then continuing for weeks this perennial of perfect symmetry is topped by hazy black inflorescences that appear from a distance as thick black smoke. It forms great colonies in moist locations in the wild, and appreciates the same conditions in gardens. This plant does best in part shade to full sun, and needs protection from slugs and snails.

ZONE 4

Viola 'Sorbet Black Delight'

'Sorbet Black Delight' viola

The viola, a cherished mainstay of gardens, is one of the very few flowers that is found in true black, like the cultivar 'Sorbet Black Delight'. Smaller than the more emotive pansies, these violas are in no way somber despite their inky hue. Their small faces evoke a playfulness, instead, like children wearing Halloween masks. As a true perennial it prefers cooler temperatures, rich soil, and average amounts of water to do its very best. 'Sorbet Black Delight' will reach eight inches, is ideal in autumn containers, and will often bloom through Halloween or until a very hard freeze.

ZONE 5

Vitis vinifera 'Purpurea'

Purple-leaved grape

ZONE 6

Perhaps no vine conjures the image of old-world sophistication as the classic wine grape. 'Purpurea' is a selection of that grape that has foliage tinted rich merlot red. A vigorous vine that attaches itself to structures with coiling tendrils, it will reach twenty feet tall over time and form a handsome gnarled trunk. Pair with white-flowered vines such as *Clematis viticella* 'Alba Luxurians', or in milder areas *Solanum jasminoides* for an elegant airy contrast. Autumn color is a festive display of red and orange. This vine produces clusters of deep purple grapes which are edible, but primarily ornamental.

Weigela 'Java Red'

'Java Red' weigela

ZONE 4

In its past incarnation weigela was a shrub relegated to old-fashioned landscapes, but 'Java Red' has propelled it to new heights of popularity. Rich chocolate-burgundy foliage forms an ideal foil for the deep red tubular flowers that appear in an initial large flush in late spring and then sporadically throughout the season. More compact than typical varieties, it matures to an eight-foot-tall vase-shaped shrub. It is easy to grow in almost any soil, but does best with average amounts of water in summer. 'Java Red' shows well among the tall feathery spires of miscanthus or carefree perennials like daylilies.

Zantedeschia 'Schwarzwalder'
'Schwarzwalder' calla lily

The pure, sleek simplicity of the calla lily has captured the hearts of gardeners and passionate lovers alike. 'Schwarzwalder' (German for "black forest") is a decadent chocolate-colored selection with just a hint of infused cherry. A slim spathe wraps gently around and folds into the shape of a fluted goblet. Its very tip is pointed outward in an erect display. It is ideally suited to florist culture, but may be grown in the ground in mild climates, and likes rich, well-amended soil with ample water during the growing season. 'Schwarzwalder' can reach an imperial eighteen inches tall.

ZONE 9

USDA WINTER HARDINESS ZONES

AVERAGE ANNUAL MINIMUM TEMPERATURE

Temperature (deg. C)	Zone	Temperature (deg. F)
Below −45.5	1	Below −50
−42.8 to −45.5	2a	−45 to −50
−40.0 to −42.7	2b	−40 to −45
−37.3 to −40.0	3a	−35 to −40
−34.5 to −37.2	3b	−30 to −35
−31.7 to −34.4	4a	−25 to −30
−28.9 to −31.6	4b	−20 to −25
−26.2 to −28.8	5a	−15 to −20
−23.4 to −26.1	5b	−10 to −15
−20.6 to −23.3	6a	−5 to −10
−17.8 to −20.5	6b	0 to −5
−15.0 to −17.7	7a	5 to 0
−12.3 to −15.0	7b	10 to 5
−9.5 to −12.2	8a	15 to 10
−6.7 to −9.4	8b	20 to 15
−3.9 to −6.6	9a	25 to 20
−1.2 to −3.8	9b	30 to 25
1.6 to −1.1	10a	35 to 30
4.4 to 1.7	10b	40 to 35
Above 4.4	11	Above 40

PHOTOGRAPHY CREDITS